A JOURNEY FROM EMPLOYMENT TO ENTREPRENEURSHIP

A BOOK TO TURN A GREAT IDEA INTO A SUCCESSFUL BUSINESS

SAURABH GOEL

ISBN 979-888530983-7

This book is dedicated to my parents for believing in me and encouraging me to follow my dreams.

Contents

CHAPTER ONE

INTRODUCTION

This book is based on my own last 10 years of work experiences, studies, and learnings. This is the journey that I experienced and most of the entrepreneurs' experience in their life. Some give up at any stage and some refuse to give up and become successful entrepreneurs.

There was only one goal in my life to do some big business. But there was no one in the school, in the college, in family, or in surrounding society, who could show the right path which leads to my goal. Wherever, the only goal of studying was told a good job.

There is no theory in academic that teach how to be financially free at a young age. They teach you to get a degree, do a job, save your money and invest it in a retirement plan and leave the world.

When you know the goal but the path is unknown, then the journey becomes a little difficult. At first, I do not understand where to start the journey. Because of this, one has to go on the wrong paths, some wrong turns have to be taken, but if you have faith in your mind, you get the right path. In this book, you will read a journey that makes an entrepreneur a successful entrepreneur.

So, that you can make your path and share your journey with others.

If you think this is the book only for those who want to do business or own his business. No, this is the book for everyone because it relates to everyone's any part of their life. Whether you are a business owner, doing a job, or student, or a retired person you will relate.

The goal of this book is not simply to try to fix the things that are not working. Rather, I wrote this book as a guide to focus on and amplify the things that do work.

There are other people like me in this world who want to start their own business, they also have great ideas but they don't know how to start, where to start. This is the reason 95% population work for 5% population. This book will change your mindset and you will learn what 5% of people do.

This is not a long book you can read it easily. I tried to explain my point by some examples or by true stories. Some topics in this might offend you, or challenge you because they violate the old beliefs that you created over time.

We are always taught to go to school get good marks, take admission to a good college, get a degree, get a good job, work 9 to 5 job, get a salary, invest in some mutual funds or into some banking schemes then after 30 40 years you will be rich. This book denies all these teachings taught by your parents, your teachers, or your society.

I read lot of books by different authors from different countries. I found most important thing that it does not matter from which country or which religion you are belonging, somewhere you relate to the author's point of view.

I read a lot of books by different authors from different countries. I found the most important thing that it doesn't matter from which country or which religion you belongs, somewhere you relate to the author's point of view.

The reason is the common human psychology and behavior. The common human psychology never changes whether you belong to any country. This book consists the common human psychologies and behaviors. In some parts of the book, you will relate completely. Note the key takeaways, learn the lesson and make your path.

CHAPTER TWO

Self - Realization

"It's time to start living the life you have only imagined. - Henry James"

There are many realization days in life. But sometimes a day also comes when we realize — "What we are doing with our life? Are we doing any justice with our life? Or we are just living to survive only."

One day, I was sitting at the counter of my shop and I realized the same that what I am doing with my life. My dream was to become a successful businessman but what I am doing is not a business. If it is then why I am not happy with it. I was having a shop where I sold food products.

That day I was upset and thinking about a job person that he is better than me. I never wanted to job because I never wanted a 9 to 5 routine, go to the office come back home, and work for someone's dream. But I found a job person is better than a self-employed especially a shopkeeper whose routine is hectic than a job person.

A Shop keeper works more than a job person. Have more than 12 hours duty and no holidays and worse busier on festivals. He thinks many times to go anywhere for holidays but do not go. You can say he rarely goes on holiday.

My realization was the same. No doubt there is money in business more than a job but there is no time for the self. We called it self-employed but we are self slaves.

Whatever you are doing is right or wrong, the best way to know that where do you see yourself after 5 years in that field. If you see yourself in a better place and you are happy then what you are doing is fine. If you don't see it then it is wrong.

I did the same and I saw that what I am doing is not right. I found myself not happy after 5 years. And the path I have chosen is very slow. My dreams can never be fulfilled on this path. Then what is the way to get financial freedom, where I have a lot of money as well as a lot of time?

I did schooling for 14 to 15 years and 4 years in my B.tech degree. In my almost 19 years academic career, nobody talked about entrepreneurship. All I heard only — "Study, if you want a good job. You have to score good marks so that you can get admission to a good college." A good college means where you can get a job after passing.

The irony of education is that even after studying from business school, people look for jobs. Even in business school or college, nobody encourages you to do business. They encourage you only for a job.

Nobody talks about how someone can be financially free at a young age. My decision was clear from my childhood that I will do business but did not know which one. For me, the meaning of business was your boss.

Before doing business I used to think that I should do a job for a few years so that I can get some experience. But later I found out experience comes from what you do in life, not from what you do in a job. I also realize you don't need a job to get experience.

I remembered an anecdote that I may have forgotten. That story deepened my realization. Once upon a time, I went shopping in a market with my father. There we took some clothes and left them for alternation. We said that tomorrow we will take it. On this shopkeeper told they have a market strike tomorrow against the administration. So tomorrow will be close.

The administration had asked to keep the market closed for one day in a week. The market people were against it so that they could keep the shop open for 7 days. On this statement, my father said that "You should take a day off so that you can also spend what you are earning. What will you do of all that money if you will not have time to spend?"

That thing clicked me and made me think. At that time I decided in my mind that whatever work I will do, I will take care that I have money as well as time. But whatever work I did, I did not get all this.

The day I had this in my mind, I started looking for the right path on the Internet. In the search for the right path, I was introduced to Network Marketing. I was convinced by the plan of network marketing. I thought I found the work that I was looking for. Every network marketer says Network Marketing is a system-building program that helps you in financial freedom.

In the end, I found Network Marketing is not a full-proof financial freedom program. It does not make your system, it makes the system of the Founder of a particular Network Marketing company. In the chapter on System Building, I explained why Network Marketing is not a System Building program for the person who joined the network marketing not founded.

Network Marketing business played the most important role is to understand what business is. What is the actual meaning of System Building? It was a turning point in the journey from employment to entrepreneurship. In network marketing, people motivate you towards your dreams. Their motivational sessions helped me in awakening those dreams which were hidden somewhere. I got the purpose of my life.

After walking a lot in different ways I found the right way that finally helped me to find the work I wanted to do. A way to complete the journey from employment to entrepreneurship.

Here I am sharing whatever I learned and the way to build the system so that you can also come into the cater of entrepreneurship.

CHAPTER THREE

REAL WEALTH

"*The ultimate wealth is having the free time to live how you want to live. - Unknown*"

If you ask for the definition of wealth you will get different answers. Societies definition for wealth is a lot of money, a luxurious home, a luxurious car, charted plane, exotic trips, expenses watches, branded cloths, etc. Wealth is defined by the lavish luxury life.

How do you define wealth?

Well, real wealth is you have time plus money. So that you can make a choice that you want to do. Wealth is not embodied in a luxurious car or home but in the freedom to know that you can buy it.

Apart from breathing, drinking water, and eating food, if all is more important in life is time and money. The person gives his time to earn money and he gives money to get a good time.

I have seen many such people who worked hard to fulfill their dreams and earned a lot of money. Build their dream home and buy everything that a sedentary lifestyle should have. But they do not have time to enjoy all.

What is the use of a swimming pool at home when there is no time to swim in it, what is the use of a snooker table when there is no time to play? In actual they are not living their dream, but their dream is living them. They are trapped in lifestyle illusion. The irony of looking wealthy is that it is an enemy to real wealth: it destroys freedom, it destroys health, and it destroys relationships.

Some people say "they do not like materialistic things that's why they do not want to earn more. Whatever I have, I am happy in it."

There may be two reasons for this statement, one is they do not know how to make wealth and the second is they afraid to comet from their comfort zone. So that they make excesses.

If you do not like materialistic things it's ok, make money, make time and make a choice of what you want to do. But making excuses is not the right decision and not real wealth.

There are only two limitations in a journey of life - Time and Money.

Time

You must have seen that people spend their time in a line for hours to get free. Some keep waiting for a long time to save some money. People think money is limited and time is in abundance. If it was not so, then they would have spent the time thoughtfully and the money by not thinking so much.

> "*Time is not a commodity, something you pass around like a cake. Time is the substance of life. When anyone asks you to give your time, they're asking for a chunk of your life. - Antoinette Bosco*"

People value their time at zero. It's free. They are convinced that time is abundant and in endless supply. They feel like they'll never die.

> "*When time is wasted as a lifestyle choice you will be stranded in places you do not want to be. - Unknown*"

People waste their time watching TV playing video games, surfing the internet, on mobile phones. Because they feel life sucks. Life needs an escape.

It is believed that a normal person spends the precious 10 years of his life in things that are not necessary for him. He could spend these 10 years building a system for him. Once a system is created, he can do whatever he wants for the rest of his life.

Money is an abundant resource while time is not. You can always acquire more money, but you cannot defy mortality.

I remember a very interesting anecdote which I had read somewhere. "Once a man goes to the bank of a river to catch fish. By the time he reaches there, it is already dark. He thinks why don't I wait for morning.

He sits there and waits for the morning to come. For his time pass, he takes out stones from a stone bag kept nearby and starts pouring them in the river.

The night passes by pouring stones and it becomes morning and only one stone is left in his hand. As soon as there is a little light, he sees that he has a diamond in his hand, not a stone. He realizes that the stones he had thrown in the river overnight were all diamonds. He feels sad that he shed all the diamonds in the river because of the darkness."

In actuality, these diamonds are the time which people consider as stones and waste them on meaningless things. By the time they realize this, it is too late. That's why I say, stay for a while and see if you too are putting the diamond in the river as a stone. If so, then there are still many diamonds left in that bag, which means there is still time to think about something.

Time is the coin of your life. It is the only coin you have, and only you can determine how it will be spent. Be careful lest you let other people spend it for you. - Carl Sandburg

Money

Time alone is not enough you also need money for balance. Most people are working for money. If you are going to the office daily 9 to 5 then just to earn money. But even after earning money, many people do not get happiness, so their perception of money has changed.

Wrong Perception about Money

> *"Money can't buy happiness, but it can make you awfully comfortable while you're being miserable. - Clare Boothe Luce"*

You must have often heard this statement *"Money does not buy Happiness"* or you must have said it yourself. Those who say this they already concluded they will never have money. People also say "more money is not good". These are not their statement they heard from somewhere and repeat it.

In actual they do not know about real wealth.

Money does not buy happiness but it buys the freedom to watch your kids grow up, to pursue your craziest dreams, to make a difference in the world, and freedom to build relationships. Happiness has nothing to do with money but it has to do with freedom.

Money buys your time and time can buy happiness. So money can buy happiness too. If you have money and time then you can do anything that makes you happy.

Time + Money

There are 4 types of people in the world. First, those have time but not money, second, those have money but not time, third those have neither have money nor time, and last those have money and time as well.

Now you can relate it with the people around you in different professions. You will find first, second, third types of people are very common, and the fourth type of people are very rare.

This fact also made me think. Whatever I did, I got stuck in the first 3 categories.

A simple rule of life was understood. If life is to be lived well then it is necessary to have both money and time. If you have money and there is no time to spend it, then that money has no use.

Being rich means everyone's own. Most people think that becoming rich means that they can buy the things they like. Earlier I used to think the same. But later I understood that along with money, it is also important to have time. So that you can do whatever you want whenever you want.

What do you think? People like Jeff Bezos, Elon Musk, or Mark Zuckerberg are working because they have to work only then their basic needs will be accomplished. No way. Rather, those people are doing what they want to do.

A short story that will make you think too. This is the story of a squirrel and a lion.

"A lion lived in a forest. A squirrel used to work near him. The squirrel was very hardworking. She used to complete all her work on time with great sincerity and hard work.

The squirrel was also very happy to work excessively, because its master, the king of the jungle, the lion, had promised to give her ten sacks of walnuts in return for completing the task. The squirrel thought that after getting ten sacks of walnuts, her future would be bright. Then she will never need to work again.

The work was long. Despite this, the squirrel was engaged in completing the daily work.

While working, when the squirrel got tired and thought that she should take some rest in the shade of the tree, but she stops, she reminds at that very moment that the lion would give her ten sacks of walnuts. And she will get the nut only when she completes the work. Thinking this, she went to work again.

When she saw squirrels like her running and playing on the tree, she felt like playing too. Spend time with her friends. Taste the sweet and sweet fruits of the tree together with them and rest in the shade of the tree with everyone.

But when she remembered ten sacks of walnuts, she stop sand gather her mind, and start doing her work again.

Time passed. At last, the day came when the squirrel finished her work.

The lion king of the jungle was very honest. According to his promise, the lion gave ten sacks of walnuts to the squirrel and set her free.

The squirrel was very happy to get the fruits of her hard work. But the very next moment she became sad. And sitting near the sack started thinking that what is the use of this nut for me now? My teeth have worn out after work. How do I eat them? I am old now too. During the days of jumping, I kept working thinking that my future would be better if I got ten sacks of walnuts. I will live life comfortably, but now there is no life left, so what will I be able to use for them. How many days will I be able to eat them? After me, someone else will take it without any effort."

This story tells the reality of the life of today's man.

A person gives up his desires and spends his whole life earning money by doing a job and business. He does this because he is worried about his future. That's why he thinks day and night only about earning money.

Even if any desire comes into his mind, he avoids it. If you ever feel like going on a holiday then you think you will go later. As long as there is enthusiasm in the body, it loses in making the future. A future that is just a fantasy. Which he has never even seen. That too whether his life is that long or not. But still, he is always worried about tomorrow.

In a job person always think about his retirement plans. He starts earning at the age of 25 to 30 and starts saving money for retirement, for his children. He always thinks about what will happen after retirement if he will not invest in any retirement plan. So he is always in survival mode.

Time passes and that person gets old one day and retires from his work. The money earned by him by killing his desires throughout his life is lying in the form of a bank balance. Now in that state, his body has also lost the ability to enjoy the pleasures of that wealth.

Often it is also seen that his right to the money earned by that person also seems to have been lost. Because the claimant of that money becomes someone else. That means the kids have grown up.

Then what is the use of such money, such as bank balance? To earn which a person loses his whole life. And could not even use that money in return.

Retirement

When someone says to think about retirement what do you see in your subconscious mind?

An old man reading a newspaper on his chair. Do you see any young man when someone say you to imagine a retirement scene?

People invest more than half of their life into a job just to retire at the age of 60-65 so that they can enjoy that money they earned. How uninspiring is this? The work you are doing takes 40 to 50 years of your life to make you financially free, is it worth it?

If you think that you will accumulate money for 50-60 years and enjoy your life after retirement, then let me tell you that by then your excitement will be over. Your mindset will be like what to do, by doing all this. This is not the age for doing all these things. At the time of buying a car, they have a statement that a car is a car. Ford and Rolls Royce both have 4 tires.

Observe or survey by yourself how many people doing after retirement at age of 60-65 that they want to do in their younger age. But they give up on that because they think they do it later after retirement. I can bet you, you will find 1 person out of 100 people or maybe 0.

These type of people never enjoy their life and their mindset does not allow them to enjoy it because of the programming of their minds. They programmed it so strongly in many years. A program took 66 days to become a habit, now think what 30-40 years will do.

This is not necessary you have to retire at 60 to 65. You can retire at any age. For that, you have to seed a money plant. The fruit from that money plant will be passive income. If you want to retire young with good health and have a lot of time to do what you want you to need to change your path.

But which path? What should be done so that we can retire at an early age?

To get its answer it becomes important to understand various ways of earning. So that you can choose the right way that gives you money and time as well.

CHAPTER FOUR

VARIOUS WAYS OF EARNING

"The best way to make money in business is not to think too much about making it. - Henry Ford"

After knowing what is real wealth, it becomes necessary that what is the right way to get this wealth. There are two basic ways by which anyone can earn; Employment and Entrepreneurship.

Employment includes job and self-employment. Entrepreneurship includes business and investment. These are four legal ways to make money. I have mentioned legal ways because it must be coming to your mind that money can be earned in another way also. Like corruption, stealing, by committing any scam. But these are not the legal ways.

You will be surprised to know that 95% of the people are in the employment category and 5% are in entrepreneurship. Means 95 % of people are employees and self-employee. 5 % are entrepreneurs, producers, innovators, visionaries, creators, and investors. The biggest thing is that 95% of the world's total wealth is owned by 5% of the people and only 5% of wealth is owned by 95% of people.

Often we feel that what the majority of people do, is the right way. Because of this, more crowds start joining the majority. It is not that this ratio is present only in today's time, but it has always been so and always will be.

Think yourself, if 95% of the people doing what, were right, they would have the largest share of the world's wealth. But it is not so. After all, why do 5% of the people have the largest share of the world? To understand this, one has to understand all the ways of earning.

Employment

If you work for someone like a job or do some work of your own like your own shop, or any profession like doctor, chartered accountant, player, advocate, actor, singer, teacher, that's all come in the employment category.

Employee

The first way to earn money is a job. Most of the people in this world are job seekers. It is not that you cannot become rich by doing a job, if you invest your earned money in some good plans, then you can become rich. Or you can earn good money by reaching a higher post.

But reaching the higher post is not in your hand it's a game of luck. I do not believe in the word Luck but in the job, everything is not in your hand. Even how much you will last at your job is also not in your hand. There are very less people who got the job package like Sunder Pichai CEO of Google and other CEO of a big company.

But if a company pays you so much, then it also takes that much time from you instead. There is no doubt that you earn a lot by reaching this level, but you still do not have time.

Most people prefer a job because of security. Because they got monthly salary and have not risked of losing money like a business. That's true job are secure than business but you can earn limited in the job because you have limited time.

Doing a job is not a method of making wealth but a method of earning income.

The financial destination does not exist in the life of a jobby person. As soon as the salary of the month comes, it is spent in loan installments, credit card payments, electricity bills, household expenses, children's fees, etc. According to the report, around 70% of people under the age of 55 have zero net worth or negative net worth.

> "*By working faithfully 8 hours a day, you may eventually get to be the boss and work 12 hours a day. - Robert Frost*"

In a job, you sell your life for money. If you work, you get paid. If you don't work, you don't get paid. You have no control over your income. If you don't control your income, you don't control your financial plan. If you don't control your financial plan, you don't control your freedom.

There is neither safety nor security in a job. In the covid-19 pandemic, we saw how safe and secure the jobs are. Many people lost their job and lost people who were doing jobs. After that, the financial condition of the family went from bad to worse. The coming time is of Artificial Intelligence where man work will be reduced and machines will take their place.

Artificial Intelligence

The time to come is of artificial intelligence. The man work will be reduced and they will be replaced by robots. Already done in a lot of fields. But after a few years, this ratio will increase further. It means to say that in the coming time job opportunities will decrease instead of increase.

The human capacity to do any work is limited. He can do limited work in limited hours in a day. But the machine can work 24 x 7 without stopping. You do not need to pay them every month. Then why a company will hire someone to do the work.

That's what an entrepreneur does. He invents something that reduces human efforts, time, expenses, and increases productivity and income.

Self Employee

The second way to earn money is by doing something my own which is called self-employee. Like opening a shop, store, restaurant, small clinic, tuition institute, a CA firm, any professional like lawyer, doctor, actor, sportsperson, singer, etc come into self-employment.

You know what, self-employment is a trap. You do everything by own and you earn until you are working. If you get a break from work you also get a break from money. That's why self-employed are always stuck in the trap and do not make time for themselves.

You know guys most of the people are either employed or self-employed. When a job worker feels that he should do something of his own, then when he starts doing something of his own, he falls into the trap of self-employment. Then he feels he was better in the job because there is some time for himself so he gave up and move to the job again.

95% of people are employees or self-employees. They are the people who belong to the A, B, C categories that I mentioned in the chapter on real wealth. There are only 5% of people who have both time and money.

If you own a shop and few team members working for you then you are not a business owner you are a self employee or a short business owner. Because the business owner is those who build the system and that system work for them. Whether they work or not they still earn money. There are many examples like Bill Gates, Elon Musk, Mark Zuckerberg, Ambani, Warren buffet, etc.

You must have never heard that any actor or footballer or cricketer became the richest person in the world. They are rich but not the richest. The reason is Time.

In the best-selling book "The Monk Who Sold His Ferrari by Robin Sharma", the author tells the story of Julian Mantle. Julian Mantle had a lot of money. He had a luxury car Ferrari, a luxury home. He had everything a normal person would want. But he didn't have time. Used to work 18 hours. Even after having so much money, there is no time to eat properly, no time for family. To realize it he had to face a heart attack.

My question is why people wait for the trauma, or for some miss happening to realize that earning money is not enough you need time to balance your life.

You give your 5 or 6 days to earn 1 or 2 days that we call weekends. Most of the people give their 7 days in return for zero. Now think if you give someone $5 and get $2 in return. How does that deal? Is it a fair deal or unfair?

The fair deal will be when you give $5 and get $5 or more of it. Work for 5 to 10 years, young retire so that you will have to enjoy your life. That is the real wealth and the balance of life.

I had understood one thing which most people do not understand and remain trapped in this trap.

The thing is all we have limited time. Means all have 24 hours in the day. There is no one on the planet those have 30 or 50 hours. So, you can work for a limited time a day. You may work for 8 to 10 hours or 12 hours and a maximum of 16 to 18 hours. You can't work for the whole 24 hours because you need time to rest also.

If you work for a limited time then you will also earn limited. If you are growing in the job sector you will stop at saturation point and you will not pay more than that. Even you are self-employed you will also reach a saturation point but you can not say you will be the richest person in the world because you can work for a limited time only even you open your shop for 24 hours.

Most of the shopkeepers think to extend their business without knowing how to multiply time in business and they are trapped into another trap. The business extension makes them super busy.

Business Extension is not a bad thing but If you are doing extensions just to increase income its makes you super busy. I have seen a lot of people who have not to time even to take lunch comfortably. They earn good money and invest this money in properties and real estate. But no time for lifestyle. What is the use of that money when you have no time for your health? I think they earn money to fill the pockets of doctors.

Not expand business just to multiply income. Multiply your time too by building a system. If you just multiply income not time then you also multiply your workload and your tension. That's the reason people suffer from anxiety and depression.

Tiny habitats create tiny wealth. Think big, nationally, and globally. To make millions, you must affect millions. That does not happen in a small store on the main street, but in hundreds of stores across the country. Sell millions, help millions, serve millions, impact millions.

If you create successful retail and franchise it to 100 entrepreneurs around the country or 1000 entrepreneurs around the world, you can reach millions. Like MacDonalds did.

Another way of earning is entrepreneurship.

Entrepreneurship

Here my meaning by entrepreneurship is not only businessman, it also includes producers, innovators, visionaries, creators, authors, and investors.

Business

Here business means a system that works for you, not you work for the system. You just build the system. When more than 500 people work for you then you come into the business category. Like Mark Zuckerberg founder of Facebook, Jeff Bezos founder of Amazon, Elon Musk founder of Tesla, Bill gates founder of Microsoft, and Jack Ma founder of Alibaba.

There is a huge difference between a self-employed and a businessman. A self-employed person wants to be the best in his field, on the other hand, a business person often is looking for other people who are the best in their field to join his team. You can say self-employed is the smartest person on his team, on the other hand, a businessman makes a team of smart people.

Innovators, visionaries, creators, and authors also come into entrepreneurship because they also make passive income. They do not need to work for money like employees or self-employee. They create content and innovate techniques and devices that they earn for lifetimes. Like an author take royalty for his book. In chapter 'System Building' you will earn how these things help in system building.

Investors

Investors are those who invest their money in various projects, stocks, mutual funds, gold coins, cryptocurrency, shares, businesses, or real estate. Their goal is money work for them instead they work for money.

An investor is a real financial-free person. He just create the system by just investing money and that system create money for him. He has time and money as well. I find a rental income is also a good idea. In that, you just need to invest and earn a fixed income on monthly basis or annually. You do not need to do anything, you just earn.

In today's world, we all need to be investors. Investment requires money. If you have money then invest. If not then earn by 3 ways of earning that I told earlier and then invest.

You can see the difference between employment and entrepreneurship. One more difference that makes entrepreneurs the richest persons in the world is the saturation point.

Saturation Point

We see there is a saturation point in job and short business. If you start a job with 5 digit salary, later it might be 6 or 7 digits. You will finish at some saturation point. Same in short businesses there is also income stop at some saturation point. Sometimes the scale goes down instead of increasing because of competition.

Have you ever heard that the employee of such a company became the richest man in the world? Leave aside the matter of the world, he cannot become the richest man of that company. Can an employee be richer than his employer? Yes, only if he cheats his employer.

There is no job where you can say one day you will be the richest person in the world. I am not making you negative for a job, but I am making you aware of a bitter truth.

But in entrepreneurship, there is no saturation point. The more your database or customer base will increase, the more your income will increase. The more you will leverage your time, your earning will increase.

Entrepreneurs like Jeff Bezos, Elon Musk, were millionaires now they are billionaires, and there is no time they will be the first trillionaires of the world. Meant to say there is no saturation point in entrepreneurship.

What entrepreneurs do that makes them the wealthier. They have both time and money. The thing that makes them the wealthier is system building. They made the system that works for them, they do not work for the system.

CHAPTER FIVE

SYSTEM BUILDING

"Either make your system work for you or you will always have to work for someone else's system. - Saurabh Goel"

Before proceeding further think for a moment that time and money are not an issue in your life. You can do whatever you want to do. You can go wherever you want to go. You will be able to spend quality time with your family. You will be able to roam anywhere without any tension. Imagine you are free from the trap of *"go-to office come back home."*

It may seem like a fairy tale to many people. But this is a reality for many people. You also know these types of people I mean people who have time and money as well.

Do you know why most people think this is just a dream because they feel that it is impossible for them or they feel that they are not worthy of it?

Let me clear one thing, neither is all this impossible and you are not unworthy of it, it is your misconception. You just need to learn some facts that help in building a system.

Knowledge is the First Step

There is a short story about a man who lived in a cave in a jungle for a long time. One day he decided to make a wooden home so that he can settle his family. To make a wooden home he needs to cut trees so he thinks to buy a saw. He went to buy a saw at a local hardware shop.

He said, "I need a best saw by which I can cut trees easily and money is not an issue, give me a best saw". The shopkeeper brought a saw from his store and said this is the best saw in the market and will cut trees like a knife cut butter. I guarantee you it will cut a month's timber in a day. If it does not I will refund your money.

That man paid the money and got excited to make his wooden home. He moved to the jungle.

Exactly one month later that man came to a shopkeeper and said I want to return this saw and want my money refund. His condition was very bad. He looked like he hadn't slept since weeks.

Shopkeeper asked "what happened to you? You are looking Terrible!"

The man said "you sold me the cheap saw. You said that with the help of this I will cut wood for a month in one day. But I have been using it for a month and could not cut even a single day's wood in a month. I want my money back!"

The shopkeeper apologized and said "Sure, I will return your all money as I promised. Let me check this saw what's wrong in it."

The shopkeeper pulled the rope of the saw and it started with a roaring sound. The man jumped back out of fear and said "what was it?"

Did you get my point from the story? If you do not know chainsaws and try to cut trees without them turning on. So what will happen? Same that happened with that man. Everyone has the tool that is Mind. You just need to learn how to use it. Most people work without getting any knowledge and they do not get the desire results.

"Knowledge is the first step and action is another."

How to Build a System?

The first thing you need to learn is how to multiply your time.

Time Multiplication

Think, if a car manufacturer make a car by himself, he can keep the 100% profit. But he knows he can make only one or two cars in a year. So, he leverages his time and talent by giving training to his employees. If he leverages 1000 people that means he build 1000 or 2000 cars in a year.

This is the simple mathematical formula that was taught to us in school but the business world implemented it.

Normally people work for 8 hours a day. For that they get a salary. Now think about the company owner for whom 500 people are working. They work 8 hours a day. That means 500 x 8 = 4000 hours of work has been done for a company owner in a day.

Like I told you, *"either be happy in doing what you can do in the limited time you have or multiply your time by leveraging."*

Power of Leveraging

Often I have seen people, they want to do everything by themselves. They think, what to do by hiring someone. Most people don't like to take risks they just want to be safe. For this reason, they remain trapped in a trap of self-employment. Some people don't even know what is Leveraging all about.

Leveraging is simply a way to light your work. You use it in your everyday life by using machines. Traveling 40 KM journey by car instead of walking is also the form of leveraging. Because you simply save your time as well as your efforts.

There are many examples from which you can learn what is the power of leveraging to build the system. Just by leveraging others' time and manpower, you can build your system. But the question is "how to leverage others' time and man power?". There are some ways and systems that can help in understanding the power of leveraging.

Team Building

One day I was sitting in my garden and I noticed a honey bee hive on a tree. I kept on observing her while sitting. Some flies were already sitting on it, some were coming, some were going. It was completely teamwork.

Seeing all this, it came to my mind that it is difficult for a single bee to make such a big hive. Her whole life will pass but she will not be able to make such a big hive. And secondly, all the flies do not make honey from the same flower, they collect the juice from all different flowers, then honey is made.

Same in the business world. To make an empire you need to build a team. When different people with different skills and talents work together then an actual system is made. This is also called collective intelligence.

If you want to understand a lesson of collective intelligence just once observe the ants. An ant alone is nothing but in a group they can do many things. They work in groups and use collective intelligence. If you also use this principle of collective intelligence you can build the system that will work for you.

Another factor of team building is synergy. It also plays a very important role in system building.

Synergy

While gardening, I learned one thing that when a plant is alone, it grows less. But if there are too many plants together, they grow more. This is the power of synergy. If you think your business will grow more by doing everything by own then I will say you are wrong. Your business grows better when you work as a team.

If you put two pieces of wood together, they will hold much more than the total weight held by each separately. The whole is greater than the sum of its parts. One plus one equals three or more.

Just as you need a lot of ingredients to make a dish and all the ingredients have a different value in themselves. Similarly, to make a big system, you need different people with different skills and different values. When you synergize you grow better.

Some Business Systems Ideas

Some business systems Ideas are used by people in different fields. You have seen all the systems around you but maybe not observed their power. But after reading all you will get to know how someone became or become rich so fast.

Education System

I don't know whether you ever heard this dialogue from your parents or not but I have heard it many times. Why did you study when you didn't want to job? You were educated only so that you can do the job.

It means to say that our society itself tells that education is never meant to make you rich. Nobody tells us that you too can make your system. That's all we are told, education means a job.

Schools, colleges, and universities are the kind of system building. This is impossible for the school owner to teach all the students of all classes by itself. So that he leverages teachers to teach students. Make administration operate all the system.

The wonderful thing is that where you study is a system in itself, but it never inspires you to make your system. Always motivated for the job.

Teachers teach only whatever they learned many years before. How they can teach you about limitless belief when they have limited belief. A person with limited belief cannot give a lesson to think out of the box. This is not the universal truth that all teachers are the same. But my only concern is how someone can teach you about something he never experienced.

A professor who is doing a job in business College, how he can teach you about system building when he never made any system and never gone to make any. He is himself just a part of a system. That's the reason a teacher never talks about business, not talk about system building. He always says to study and get the degree to get the job. College seems like a 4 to 5 years brainwashing program. Nobody talks about entrepreneurship, all just talk about the job.

But no problem, you can make your own system by looking at the education system. Think if there is only one teacher in the school, then it is difficult for him to teach all the children. That's why the school owner hires teachers of different subjects. He hires different staffs for different operations. By using the power of leveraging he build the system that is now working for him.

Content System

The content system is the information system. That information can be linked to many other systems, such as the Internet and physical distribution. In the world of information, you can make content by writing books, blogs, by creating courses and videos.

The latest trend of content distribution has merged with computer systems. Youtube videos, content on social networking sites like Instagram, Facebook, Pinterest, ebooks, blogs, online courses.

This book is a business system that has unlimited leverage in both time and money. Understand this by this analysis.

Suppose, a book takes my 500 hours in writing. After publishing, I sold 1000 copies in a month on 1 dollar profit on each book. Then the cost of my time will be 2 dollars per hour. If I sold 1lakh copies? My time will be the same but my earning will increase and the value of time too. Now the value of my time will be 200 dollars per hour.

By writing a book I made a system that can give me money for a lifetime and so on.

The book "Think and Grow Rich by Napoleon Hill" was published in 1937. It's over 100 million copies have been sold. This figure can be even more, I am telling what I read on the cover page of the book that I purchased. After 74 years, this book has not stopped selling. Rather, its sale has increased only.

Author Napoleon Hill is no longer in this world, but the royalty of this book must have gone to the account of any member of his family. This example is one of the content system.

Another example, I was listening to an interview recently, it was the interview of the son of a very famous movie director and producer. His father made a movie 50 years ago. It was not such a hit at that time. But after some time people liked that movie. Today it has been 50 years, people still like that movie, and the son of that director still gets the money.

A movie producer earns royalty for a lifetime. OTT(over-the-top) media and television pay producers to show his movie on their platforms. Similarly, a music director takes royalty on his music and a writer on the writing of the story of the movie or lyrics of the song. Poet on his poems, a photographer on his photo, and a videographer on his video.

Online courses are also one of the trending ways of content creation. People are making videos of a few hours on a particular topic and selling it on a different medium. Similarly, like book writing, it takes only a few hours or days for one time and you can earn by these courses for a lifetime.

This is the power of content. By creating content like these not only do you earn money, you also leave the legacy behind you for your family.

Computer System

Computer system or you can say software system is one of the most popular system these days. It is creating more wealth than other systems. Because it connects you with different people in different parts of the world through the internet. You can combine the two above systems that we discussed education system and content system with computers and can generate more wealth. Some online schools, colleges, universities and other online education platform are the examples of combination of education system and computer system.

Today's and upcoming time is the time of digitalization. Now all the content is available on the internet. If you can not make the content then you can provide the system for the content makers. Like Google, Youtube, Facebook, Instagram, Pinterest, Twitter, Quora, Medium, Tumblr, and many more platforms did.

You can make your E-commerce platform like Jeff Bezos made Amazon and Jack Ma made Alibaba. E-commerce is the one of best distribution systems these days. If you can't own your E-commerce system, you can use existing systems for your distribution system. As I used Amazon for the distribution of my book all around the world.

Most of the start-ups these days are either websites, web applications, or mobile applications. The ultimate goal of these applications is to give solutions to people's problems. Decreasing their efforts and providing them facilities. If you observe everything is going digitalized. Education, Meetings, Offices, Shops, Restaurants(Home deliveries), Banking, Entertainment, etc. all are available on your phone.

The power of a computer or software system is limitless. You just need an idea and execution.

Rental System

Rental System is a system that does not require any skill, talent, or education. It only needs the right investment in real estate. Make a residential or commercial property and rent it. In the rental system, your time and efforts do not attach to the income. You get checked every month by a tenant for using your property. You only leverage your money for that passive income.

The most important point that I like about the rental system is that the rental system is less risky. Because you invest in property which price increases every one or two years. There are very few chances of loss in the rental system.

Cooperation

Cooperation is people working together to achieve results or a common goal. If you look at any big company, you will get to see a hierarchy. CEO, Managing Director, Managers, Team leaders, different workers, etc. All work in cooperation to achieve a company's goal and vision.

Different partnerships are also part of cooperation. Partnerships give strength to the company. Like, Frederick Henry Royce was good at designing and manufacturing cars but not good at marketing. Charles rolls were good in marketing. So they both did partnership and made the world's most luxurious car Rolls Royce.

It seems a bit impossible to have all the qualities and skills in one person. But strength can be made by combining different human skills. Hire people of different skills and quality, then achieve your goal by their cooperation.

Franchise System

One of the best examples of a franchise system is "McDonald's".

McDonald's is founded by two brothers Richard and Maurice McDonald in 1940 as a restaurant. They realized for how long will the work from a single restaurant continue, why not do something big, why not build a system.

They got the idea and turned the company into a franchise in 1953. MacDonald's was the first who started the franchise. At that time people think that is an illegal business formula. But now you understand the power of the franchise.

You know what according to a report McDonald's is the world's largest restaurant chain by revenue, serving over 69 million customers daily in over 100 countries. McDonald's is the world's second-largest private employer with 1.7 million employees. Why I am sharing this because this shows the power of leveraging. What if they too were thinking small and working from a single restaurant?

Some people have an excuse, if McDonald's did it in the beginning, then it became successful. But many other examples those started franchise systems and they also become successful. Like Dominos, Starbucks, Pizza hut, Subway, etc. They just build the system.

Distribution System

One of the best ways for distribution is network marketing. I am not saying join network marketing and make your system. I am saying make your distribution system by using network marketing or you can say direct selling. Because by joining other network marketing systems you do not make your system. In actual you become part of others' systems. You are just the one link of the entire distribution chain.

Those who do network marketing always say it is the industry of making your system. If you join any network marketing company you not making a system you are just part of the system. The founder and owner are making his system. I also did network marketing. The first day when I joined network marketing I asked the first question to the person — "Am I the customer or business owner?". Because I joined the company by buying a product.

How someone can say himself an entrepreneur in network marketing? He has no control over products, their pricing, and compensation plan than how someone can say he is an Entrepreneur. There is only one Entrepreneur who founded that network marketing company. You are just the distributor — A part of the distribution chain.

Joining Network marketing is sales, distribution, and training, not entrepreneurship. If someone says network marketing is an Entrepreneurship business or a system Building, I disagree. If it is tell me what if the owner decides to set off his company for some reason. Then what will you do?? Nothing? Zero. What about the pipeline you made?

Stop climbing other's pyramids, start building your's pyramids.

Importance of System Building

You can now self-analyze the importance of system building. It gives you time freedom, passive income, and a way to be a millionaire. Apart from these, another special thing about system building is legacy.

Legacy

After reading all the systems, the one thing that clicks the most is that you not only create real wealth for yourself but also leave a legacy for your next generations.

Everyone thinks about their children's future. They save money so that their children can get an education and then get a job. Think, if you are working for a company and reach the highest level — CEO post in your company. Now, my question is —"Will your children start from the same post from which you retire?"

Whatever post you are on, your child will have to start from zero. He has to work same even more than you to reach the same level where you are or where you will be. You might be left the money in the bank account or properties in the name of legacy but not the time. They have to give same time what you gave in your life.

But in system building, you give a real legacy. Your children no need to start from zero. He will start from where you left and he will have more time more than you because he saves the time which you spend in building the system.

You can say a job is a marathon race where everyone needs to complete his race. On the other hand, system building is the relay race. You just pass on, they just need to start from where you finished. This small lesson teaches you big learning.

Automation Mode

Once you build a system it comes to the automation mode. Meaning whether you do some work or not, money keeps coming to you. You just need to keep eye on the system.

Understand this by an Inspirational story. This story always Inspires me.

"At the time of 1801, two friends named Pablo and Bruno lived in a village in Italy. They used to dream of becoming rich, wishing to have a lot of money, to build a big house, and to travel around the world. In those days people used to bring water from the river in buckets. One day the people of the villages decided to hire two people who could bring water from the river. Both these boys had the best opportunity to earn money.

The people of the village entrusted this task to Pablo and Bruno. Both the boys picked up a bucket and went to get water. The people of the village paid them at the rate of one penny per bucket.

Bruno was very happy after getting the money and started feeling that soon all his dreams would be fulfilled. But Pablo was not happy with this work. Both had pain in their back, they had blisters in their hands and after working all day, they did not have enough courage to go to work the next day. But they have to go to work, otherwise, they would not get the money.

But Pablo had understood on the very first day what was the use of earning such money, which did not have time for itself and have for work for money without interest. He had made up his intention that some other way would have to be thought of to bring water to the villages.

He thought why not build a pipeline from the river to the village, which would solve the problem of getting daily water. He told this plan to his friend Bruno. But Bruno did not understand this plan. He said Pablo we got a job with great difficulty, don't think too much. I can bring 100 buckets in a day. One penny per bucket means one dollar per day. I will get rich soon. Finish your pipeline talk and focus on work.

Pablo was not going to get discouraged so easily. He decided that he would bring buckets for half the day and would do the work of pipeline construction for half the day. Pablo believed in his dream and he kept on. Bruno and the people of the village also started making fun of him.

Bruno was earning twice as much as Pablo because he worked all day and Pablo only half a day. He bought a nice house, started wearing good clothes, started eating food in a good restaurant. On the other hand, Pablo would have been busy building his pipeline. Pablo did not get many results in the initial days, but he believed that one day his hard work would bear fruit.

He always remembers one thing that *tomorrow's dreams can be built only on the strength of today's sacrifice.*

It took some time but Pablo's efforts paid off and his pipeline was ready. On the other hand, Bruno had started looking old because of carrying buckets of water all day. His shoulders were bowed.

Now Pablo did not need to carry the bucket. Because of his pipeline, the village ponds were inundated. People from nearby villages also started coming to get water from his pipeline. Seeing him, he had become very rich.

Now, he had money and time too because it didn't matter if he woke up, slept, or roamed somewhere he will earn 24 hours. He builds the system that is now working for him instead of the need to work for the system.

After making the pipeline he started multiplying the time by hiring people, making partnerships so that he can build pipelines in the whole world."

Now, you can relate to what I am talking about. 95% of people are into bucket carrying world and 5% are pipeline makers. Business and Investment help you make the pipeline.

Whenever you think to start a business then ask this question to yourself — "Can this business be automated and systemized to operate while I'm absent?."

A business attached to your time is a job. That's why a small business owner is not an entrepreneur he is self-employed.

People say money makes more money. I will say it's not the truth. System building makes more money.

There are two ways to build the system — one is to copy the existing leveraging formulas and the second invent your new system making formula.

You know what is the basic difference between a businessman and an entrepreneur. A businessman copy the existing Idea and an entrepreneur invents his Idea.

To build your system you don't need an MBA, a certificate, a fancy suit, a briefcase, or an above-average tolerance for risk. You just need an idea, a touch of confidence, and a push to get started.

CHAPTER SIX

IDEA

"Everything begins with an Idea. - Earl Nightingale"

My main purpose in sharing this book with you is to help you in finding great ideas and turn those great ideas into a successful business. To become an entrepreneur you need an idea that can add value to others' life.

Value Addition

Find what value you can add to people's life. You can help them in their problem solving, or how you can save their time and money.

"Necessity is the mother of all inventions. - Plato"

As I said health, food, shelter, education, and security are the basic needs. A person works for these basic needs. Besides all of them, the more important is Time and Money. Find out how you can add value to someone's life.

Need

Most entrepreneurs fail because they build businesses based on selfish premises, and selfish premises do not yield profitable businesses; They lead directly to the trash with 90% failure.

Do not start businesses just to make money. Start businesses to make a difference in someone's life. You can make a difference in someone's life only when you fulfill their needs.

Most entrepreneurs start a business on what they love without any market study, without knowing customers' needs. After a few months, they stop doing it. Suppose a person likes to cut hair but he opens his hair cutting shop in the middle of the bald, then what is the percentage chance that that shop will run.

People do not care what you love. No one cares about your dreams, your passion. People only care about what your business can do for them. How it will help them?

Look around outside your world, stop being selfish, and help your fellow humans solve their problems. In a world of selfishness, become unselfish. Offer the world — value, and money becomes magnetized to you.

What you can do for customers?

- Make them feel better. (Entertainment, music, video games)
- Help them in problem solving.
- Educate them.
- Give them security.
- Make things easier.
- Raise a positive emotion.
- Save their time and money.

Opportunities are everywhere you just need to observe. Problems are the opportunity. Start observing you will start finding opportunities and ideas.

How an Idea can change your entire life.

Understand it by the example of Coca-Cola. Before Coke came in bottles, you had to go to the local soda fountain to enjoy the drink.

Two entrepreneurs namely Benjamin F. Thomas and Joseph B. Whitehead proposed the idea of bottling to Candler. That idea clicks on the candler and they start bottling it.

After bottling customer didn't have to go to the soda fountain to enjoy the drink because a consumer bought a stock of coke at his home. As a result, he can enjoy the refreshing drink any time of the day or night. All this is possible because of leveraging time, effort, and location.

There are many other examples also those who have ideas and they turned their idea into a successful business. Initially no one believe that these Ideas will work but they did it. Many people give up on their idea because they listen to the people more than their calling.

If someone has no idea?

> "*The best way to have a good idea is to have a lot of ideas. - Linus Pauling*"

You do not need to worry if you do have not an idea. The world is full of opportunities. To do not need a great or legendary idea to start anything. Successful entrepreneurs take existing concepts and improve them.

> "*Use what you have - so you will have what you want. - Unknown*"

When Google created the search engine, there was already Yahoo in the market. But he made a better search engine and today you know very well where Google is and where Yahoo is. Google is the most used search engine. The same myspace was already there before Facebook, but that didn't stop Mark Zuckerberg to make a Facebook.

The meaning of saying this is that you do not need to think much, just understand that when you solve the problem of other people, then your money problem will be solved by itself. Just offer the solutions to the masses for their discomfort, complaints, problems, distress, and inconvenience.

Observe

When you think about some work or focus on some goal, then your subconscious mind gives some signals. You just have to observe. Sometimes while working, bathing, shaving, gardening, cooking, driving your subconscious mind give ideas.

It often happens to me that when I am taking a bath or gardening, then more ideas come. I write down those ideas in my diary or on the notepad of the phone so that they do not skip from my mind. Many topics of this book click in my mind as this and I wrote them down.

Trust me it works. You need to give a message to your Subconscious Mind, it will revert you, just observe and pick it.

When you practice visualization Ideas start flowing into your subconscious mind. Sometimes these Ideas in the form of Intuitions, or form of some code language, or universe start meeting you with those people who will help in your journey. You need to pick these intuitions that can be turned into the biggest success.

Whatever happens with you in life, bad or good, take out its positive meaning. Because the universe is trying to give you a message you just need to decode and visualization can help you in it.

Trust on your intuition

> *"Gut feelings are your guardian angels sending you messages. - Unknown"*

When you have the biggest purpose in your life then the universe gives you intuition or ideas in your subconscious so that you can achieve that purpose. So trust in that intuition.

This is the key of all the greatest in the world. No one can deny my point that one click is needed to do something big in life. Might be that one intuition can be the click that can take you to the peak of success.

Now think, If Isaac newton ignored the apple that had fallen on his head, can we got know about gravity? Same, if right brothers haven't got the idea of making airplanes by seeing butterflies. There is a story behind everyone's success. As I shared an example of Coco-Cola. What was that an Idea clicks in their mind they trust it and write their name in the history.

It is not necessary that only an Intuition will come into mind and give you idea. You can meet a person who can give you the idea as Benjamin F. Thomas and Joseph B. Whitehead, proposed the idea of bottling to Candler. You can see anything that can click to your mind like a butterfly click to the right brothers. An idea can click while reading an article or reading a book. You just need to pick and trust the intuitions.

I will say if you have a dream you will get the Idea also to accomplish that dream. But do not give up on your dream. If you have an idea believe in it. All the achievers have not done anything extraordinary. They just trusted in their Ideas and refuse to give up despite the failure.

CHAPTER SEVEN

EXECUTION OF AN IDEA

> *"Having the world's best idea will do you no good unless you act on it. People who want milk shouldn't sit on a stool in the middle of the field in hopes that a cow will back up to them. - Curtis Grant"*

Many people have great ideas but they fail to execute them. There are some reasons why people do not execute them.

Fear of Failure

Because of fear of failure most people do not execute their idea. They think much but do nothing. They create self-doubt and make a wall of fear that stops them from executing their great ideas.

Listen to Others Opinions

Some people take the opinion of those people who are not doing anything themselves. Then those people demotivate them by telling stories of failures. People give up on their ideas without executing because they listen to more people who demotivate them.

High Competition

Some people are unable to do anything because of high competition. They feel that when everyone is doing this, if they do the same, then they will become a part of the crowd. And it is a bit difficult to move in the crowd. If there is something like this somewhere, instead of being a part of the crowd, think something for that crowd. What can you give them? There are old sayings - *"In a Gold rush, don't dig for gold, sell shovels."*

Meaning instead of getting stuck in the crowd, make a platform for the crowd. Like Amazon made E-commerce platform. Instead of opening its shop, made a platform where more people could sell their products. Same Google, Netflix, Youtube instead of making their content they made a platform where others can put their content. Instead of becoming part of the competition, they made the platform for that crowd.

There are a lot of examples like this like online food delivery applications, different types of tools to make you work easy. if your competitors have four features, you need five or 10 features.

To do something, instead of finding faults, start finding opportunities in challenges. Competition is everywhere. Just do it and do it better. If you have an idea, but someone is already doing it, just do it more better than them. Deliver great value, meet customer needs or become a better marketer.

Lack of Money

Most ideas go into vain because of a lack of money. To execute some ideas money requires. If you do have not any money not worry. Start finding investors. Some angel investors help start-ups in growing thier business.

If you want an angel investor to invest money in your start-up, then you have to execute your idea. The investor should see something in which he will invest. Just having an idea will not work, it will also have to be executed.

So, if you want to get funding for your business, get out and make your idea tangible. Give investors something they can see, touch, and feel.

Some other Doubts

Most people ask a very common question that "If it is that easy, everyone would become rich, and if all would become rich, then who will do the job?"

If everyone starts doing something of his own then who will work for us? Then how we will build the system?

And everyone keeps worrying about this, if everyone comes to know about the secret of becoming rich, then all will become rich and no one will work for them.

I tell you the fact that even after getting the world-class secret most people do not implement it. Many people read startups books, business books, get-rich books, and secret books but those who read all of them are not rich.

There are some books like *"Think and Grow Rich by Napoleon Hill"*, or *"The Alchemist by Paulo Coelho"*. Their millions of copies are sold around the world. What do you think everyone became rich after reading these, did everyone achieve their dreams.

Many people would not have read these books completely and many of those who would have read them completely would not have implemented them.

A short story will give you a better understanding of this.

The hunter does, as usual, he goes, lays the net, puts the grain and the parrots get caught in his net. He sells them by going to the market."

Now tell me, what do you understand by that story?

Yes, you thought right, those parrots took the advice but they did not implement that advice.

Most people know what is right and wrong for them. Most people also know what they should do. But there is a difference between knowing and doing.

It is written on the cigarette box that Smoking cigarettes is injurious to health and can cause cancer. But people still don't implement.

There are two reasons that why people do not implement still after knowing what is right for them and what is wrong for them.

First is they do not want to change. They feel it is difficult to come out of the old habits and feel comfortable in their old habits. Their comfort zone doest allow them to change.

Second is their conscious mind knows what is wrong or what is right but their subconscious mind is not aware of it. Subconscious Mind comes to know about anything when it happens in repetition or some old habits does not stop it.

The subconscious mind does not adopt any new habit because its old habit stops that habit.

These are the basic reasons people do not Implement. Now think if you do not implement and do not take any action then how you will change.

Not everyone can become rich or you can say can come into the 5% club. I am not saying a negative statement it is the fact. Few will get to know about all of this, few will implement, and few will reach the goal. Most people will give up in the middle of their journey.

Whatever Idea you have executed it. There is not necessary to follow anyone else rule. There is no fixed rule in business. You can make your path your own rules.

Execution of an Idea gives birth to a start-up.

CHAPTER EIGHT

START-UP

"The way to get started is to quit talking and start doing. - Walt Disney"

Your dream is clear, you have an idea too, you took the decision and committed too. Now, what to do so that your idea can turn into a successful business.

Converting an idea into a business is called a start-up. One idea can change not only your life but also the lives of many people who associate with you.

I have read some wealth-making books. They tell you everything like following your passion, starting a business, investing in real estate, making assets, and blah blah. But they address nothing else. The failure is within the "else" because the else is the rest of the formula. So this chapter is to addresses how you can make your start-up successful.

Every year many people bring something new to the market but 9 out of 10 start-ups fail. 20% start-up after 1 year, 30% after 2 years, and 50% close within 5 years.

My intention is not to demotivate you by telling these figures. It is just to tell you the possible reasons for the failure so that you do not make the same mistake that many people make.

There is no right or wrong way to start or there is no right or wrong time to start. I will say if you have an idea start as soon as possible. Sometimes later becomes never. So, take an immediate decision and do it now. As I said there is no right or wrong way to start anything, which approaches works that is right.

You know what, the first step is always is the hardest. Because you don't know what to do actually.

Database

Just understand the simplest quality or you can say the most fundamental key of any business. It is a database.

Here, database means customers and audience for whom we want to start a business. Any startup or any company is nothing without its customers and audience. That's the reason most of the companies build their database initially. They forget about their profit they just focus on the database.

If I talk about the most successful companies at present time Facebook, Google, Twitter, Instagram, Youtube, Amazon, Alibaba, Paypal, Netflix, Uber, and many more. All these companies have databases. You use Google for free, watch videos on youtube for free, use Twitter, Instagram, or Facebook to post anything for free. But these companies still making billions because of the database.

They give service, they give service, they sell world-class products just to make their customer database. Because these people know if they will have customer database or you can say audience they can sell to them. Suppose if they have a customer database of 1 lakh, chances are 10 to 20% of people will use their service.

Audience Building

Influence millions and make millions. In other words, how many lives did you touch? Who has benefited from your work, your wealth, and your handiwork? What problems have you solved?

The amount of money you have is a direct reflection of the amount of value you provide.

The first step is to make the strategy to build the audience. The best way to build the audience is through marketing and advertisement.

Marketing and Advertisement

Whenever an idea comes to mind, the first thing that comes to mind is how will you present your product in front of people? Where will the money come from for marketing and advertising?

Then we start finding the investors who can invest in your start-up. There is no harm in investing but without knowing the difference between marketing and advertisement your most money is wasted on wrong things. Secondly, after investment, you cant take your decisions freely. You have to cross-check your decision with the board of directors.

Don't worry if you do have not any money for marketing. If you provide the best service or product then people will do marketing for you that is called word of mouth promotion.

Word of Mouth

There is a lot of start-ups that never did their marketing or advertisement just by the word of mouth promotion they became the best.

Like, Facebook, WhatsApp, and Google. How did you come to know about Facebook? You will say by some of my friends. They told me to make the profile on Facebook. Same some of your friends told you to install WhatsApp or to buy anything from amazon. All these are the word of mouth promotions.

> *"If you do build a great experience, customers tell each other about that. Word of mouth is very powerful. - Jeff Bezos"*

Word of mouth promotion is not always the optimal way to do marketing. Because you have no control over that marketing. So that you have to opt for other marketing ways too.

Affiliate Marketing

The second way of marketing that is most popular these days is affiliate marketing. When you give people the opportunity of earning they will do your marketing more. If you share your profit with others they do self-promotion for you.

You know what google just provides a platform to search for anything there. But people write blogs for google because google shares its revenue with the bloggers. The same amazon also shares its profit if you refer to the product link with your friends. If they purchase something by that link you get the benefit.

Same you can use this marketing strategy for your product or service.

Referral Model - Direct Selling

Another marketing model is the referral model. That is the same as affiliate marketing but it's a little different. Because in affiliate marketing, a person earn money on one-time selling by him. But in referral mode person earn money on selling of products by their downline also. This is based on Direct selling. That we know as network marketing also. In a network marketing company, you need to create leaders who can create a team of large numbers. The larger the numbers will larger the revenue.

In direct selling, you save a lot of money that spend on advertisement, on the salary of a salesman, and distribution. This means you eliminate the chain that is between manufacturer and consumer. The product sells directly to the consumer by the manufacturer. In between consumers become your chain. They refer the product and for every sale, they get the reference amount.

Some companies like Amway, Herbalife, Natura, Tupperware, Forever Living, Avon, Oriflame, etc. are examples of direct selling companies. These companies not only made their system, but they are also giving opportunities to the people. You can sell your products and services by direct selling.

Unique and Best Services

If you have unique and best services and products you do not need to promote them. Like MacDonald have the fastest service. They try to give orders very quickly. Dominos promises to give delivery in 30 minutes. Amazon promises you to give same-day delivery or 1-day delivery. If you have the best product or service people attract to you. You do not need to go to customers.

If you have an ok product, poor customer service, and incompetent people, you can survive with powerful marketing. Like dominos commit 30 minutes delivery. Others have better pizza than dominos but dominos is best because of its powerful marketing and service.

Some more Powerful Marketing Strategies

Storytelling

The storyteller will rule the world. If you have some inspirational story to tell it impacts people. It connects with people. I have seen lots of advertisements that have some shots of stories that touch the heart and more important people also share these advertisements with others.

Generally, people skip the advertisement. They hate advertisements. If you present your product or service directly, there are chances more people will ignore it.

Understand it by your own experience. How many emails do you open when you see someone is just selling their products? In most cases, you delete these types of mail without open.

So make some stories so that they present your product or service perfectly. Using testimonials of customers also attract customers by seeing happy and satisfied customers.

Take reviews from customers and add them to your social media platform and your website. Make videos and create case studies documents.

Educate People

If you want to build a large audience then start to educate them. This strategy is not applicable for all industry but if you find something in your industry that you can educate people then educate them. When you spread knowledge to others it builds your credibility.

Suppose you are from the gardening industry then start giving knowledge about different plants, seeds, and which weather is suitable for which plant.

If you are from the food industry then start giving knowledge about different food and you can also share recipes with others.

If you are from the health industry then start giving tips on health. Take wellness sessions.

These are some examples to explain to you how you can educate others. Build your social media and start sharing videos, posts, podcasts. Write blogs articles and books. Share pieces of information that are valuable and you will slowly but surely build a loyal audience.

When you build an audience, you don't have to buy people's attention, they give it to you. This is a huge advantage.

Entertain People

Another marketing strategy is entertainment. Do you know? People preferred entertainment most on this earth. Entertainment seeks people's attention quickly. Some rare people spend more time on education. Most people spend their time on entertainment.

As I said earlier all strategy not work for all. It depends on you how you use them. I am giving you some examples if it makes sense for you and you can use that strategy for you then go for it.

You must have gone to such a place many times where you must have found some entertainment and you must have made a video of it and put it on social media. Or you must have seen many videos like this. As if you must have seen huge pizza at a restaurant. Or a challenge to finish something in a few minutes.

You must have seen a lot of places, someone gives some challenge, after completing which you get the reward. But have you ever thought about what happens if you do this? There is a branding of that product or that service.

People are entertained and they make videos, take pictures. You know very well where they put that videos and pictures. They upload that video and pictures on their social media. In this way, many companies get popularity for free and they get branding.

Think what you can try something so that it builds your audience and can generate more leads.

Be interactive

Being interactive means interacting with customers by giving them tester or trials initially. Because when they can taste it, feel it, or use it, they will more likely to buy it. You must have experienced yourself many times that many shopkeepers have made you their product test so that if you like it, you can buy it. If you have a service-based company then give a 7 or 14 days trial for your services.

Gimmick Marketing

Like beer, whiskey, pan masala, or product you can't show directly on a TV ad. So advertiser makes a trick to show these ads by showing other product.

In the name of some legal product, they endorse their brand. The intend is just to attract attention.

Pricing

Once upon a time, psychologists experimented to know about human psychology regarding pricing. They placed two shaped cakes on a counter. One round shape cake with a price of $20 and another rectangular shape cake with a price of $35.

They made the customers taste both the cakes. The cake which cost $35 was liked by everyone. Everything in it seemed perfect to everyone. While the $20 cake did not suit them so much. They felt it is not good in comparison to cake with a price of $35. Somebody said sugar is not good. Somebody said frosting is not good. Some pointed out some others problems in the cake.

But in reality, both those cakes were the same. Only their shapes were different. But due to the difference in pricing, they feel a difference in the quality of cake as well.

This experiment has let us know that the perception of people changes by looking at the pricing of a product. They think that if the thing is expensive then it must be good and if it is cheap then they start doubting its quality.

So while pricing the product or service, keep this in mind. Do not keep the price so low that its quality is doubted nor so expensive that people cannot afford it.

Be Unconventional

You must have seen many times that the pricing on a product is very low and there is a small star on it. Which shows the condition applied. Seeing its price, you are also surprised and try to know. The purpose of that is to get someone's attention. If you take someone else attention, half the battle you already won.

Observe Advertisement

Observe the ad that you watch on TV. You will get great ideas from them. Ads are made by marketing experts and creative directors. They work on human psychology and different strategists to attract people towards products or services. Start observing ads you will get some ideas that can help you in the promotion.

Edification

Edification adds value to your products and services, your business, your company, and you. It creates a positive and big image of your product and services. If you present your product and services normally in front of people its value decreases and people consider that product and service ordinary. Edification Includes:

1. Self-Edification

If you want people to choose you edify yourself. Edify yourself by telling your achievements, by your lifestyle. The reason is it's add value to you. There are chances you choose a person by seeing his achievements.

Would you like to hear a man standing on the stage and just saying his name and start speaking? Therefore, before calling any speaker on the stage, it is something told about speaker. Something is said in his praise about what he has achieved. So that there is a positive image in the mind of the audience and they listen to him with more interest. In same way edify yourself. Mention your achievements on websites or on any social media account.

2. Company Edification

If you have no numbers to edify your company, not to worry. You can fake it initially until you make it. Most companies use fake numbers like number of users, number of buyers, number of clients, number of people who like like their products. There is no harm in using fake numbers but not fake the quality of a product or service. It should be genuine. Company edification is necessary because people trust you sometimes by seeing the numbers.

3. Product and Service Edification

The biggest example to understand the edification of the product is the book itself. If the book is sold more, then its publishers write "the number of copies sold", or "bestseller book" or "international bookseller" on the book. This is the edification of the book. More chances you will buy a book just by seeing it is the international bestseller. I should read this book. That's how edification works.

As I explained in the company's edification — don't worry if you have no numbers *fake it until you make it*. Fake the numbers but not fake the quality of the product and service.

Sales

You have audience and customer leads. Now, the job of sales is to understand requirements and present the products and services. Handle the objections, make an offer, negotiate and close the deal.

When you generate leads through various strategies on the various platform then you need to get the word out, the right people will already be listening. They will buy your products and service. That's why I said there is a huge advantage of building an audience and generating leads.

Now think how much it will cost you to reach those hundred, thousand, or, millions of people. It will cost you nothing. Suppose you have a database of 1 million people. If you launch a new product or service. Then there are chances 20% of them will buy your product and service. Here, the 80- 20 rule will work. 20 out of 100 will buy definitely.

The remaining may be buy later. That is why you need to launch different products or services from time to time.

You must have seen the automobiles industry, electronic devices industry, or Software industry change their versions or model every year. They also launch new products and by-products. This is necessary for a repeat sale.

This is also an important point to understand. If you do not make changes to your product or do not launch a different product then the customer will not come again. For repeat sale changes are important.

When you create new products and new services you also create a new customer. You also make more money from existing customers.

Operations

If marketing is not consistent, you will not get leads consistently. If you will not have lead consistent, you will not have sales consistent. If a sale will not consistent, the operation will not consistent.

Once you build a consistent system then you just need to focus on operations. You do not need to do everything by own. Make the different department. Hire people for different departments and different operations.

Marketing department to generate leads, sales department to close the deals, accounts department, research, and development team to make changes in existing products and services and creating new products and services. You need a human resource department for recruitment, people development, and employee happiness.

Management

After building all the systems your job is management. Of course, you will hire managers too for managing all the departments. But you will be the managing director or CEO of your company. Your job is to provide the clarity — clarity of goals, clarity of the system, clarity of roles, and clarity of profitable business model.

Your job is exploring a new market, exploring a new partnership, and exploring new opportunities. After building the system focus on accelerating the performance.

If you want to build a business that can grow without you then make a team that is committed and competent. Build a system that is simple and sustainable. Focus on the strategies for a profitable business model.

When you focus on these ideas and take action to implement them you are on the way to creating some exciting breakthroughs in your life.

> *"What do you need to start a business? Three simple things: know your product better than anyone, know your customer, and have a burning desire to succeed. - Dave Thomas, founder of Wendy's"*

There is the hard fact that most people give up on early-stage and remain trapped in to trap of employment. On the other hand, few people make history. What makes these people successful?

You will get its answer in the next chapter.

CHAPTER NINE

PURPOSE

"If you do not have a purpose in your life, then make the purpose to find that purpose. - Saurabh Goel"

Do you know, what is the most important factor of all the achievements? — "Purpose". Many people define purpose as a Dream of life, a Desire, a compelling reason, or Why?

This is the most important chapter of this book. Because from this chapter you will get to know how an ordinary person becomes extraordinary. You know what, out of all the people who buy the book, only 10% of the people read beyond the first chapter. You are reading this chapter makes you already extraordinary.

You don't have talent, it's ok. You don't have money, it's ok. But you have dreams and passion you have more than talented and rich people and that's all matter.

Most people focus on How? How it will happen? How I will achieve it? How I will become rich?

When a person focus on "how", then he remains trapped in the trap of employment. On the other hand, entrepreneurs focus on "why".

Why it will happen? Why I will achieve it? Why I will become rich? When you focus on "why" then "How" automatically handle. You automatically get the ways, ideas, and solutions. You just need to focus on Your why! Your dream! Your purpose!

Why Purpose Needed?

Your purpose reminds you whenever you feel like giving up that why you started this journey? What will be the gains, when you will accomplish it and what will the pains if you will not accomplish it?

Suppose, you decided to go to a destination that is 500 km from your location. But somehow you do not have any transport facility to reach there. Then what will you do? Chances are you will skip the plan. Even you will not try to think of some other alternatives or try to find out the way how you can reach there. Because your why is not clear. You do not have any purpose. So, why you will try to find out how?

Now suppose the second scenario. You have to go the same destination that is 500km from your location. Same no transport facility. But your loved ones required your blood to survive his/her life. Then still, will you skip the plan?

I know your answer, you will say you will find out any way to reach there and you will reach there definitely. In the way, whenever you will lose the courage and feel like to giving up that purpose will give you the energy and motivation to stand again. That is the power of purpose.

Those who think it requires money or power to pursue their dream, are wrong. It requires an idea or you can say only just one click that can turn your life. Put aside the thought that, you need money to do anything in life. Because you don't need money to do anything, you need purpose.

Everyone has some dream in life or to achieve something in life or to become rich. But over time, the dream of most people gets blurred.

Some reasons come in the way of people's dreams

First, the society around us. We are told from childhood that the dream we are dreaming is not possible. We live in a negative society those thinking is pessimistic and they feel that dreams never come true.

If we get over it, then the fear of defeat makes our dreams blurry. There is a fear in the mind, if you fail then what will society say. They already said don't dream, dreams never come true.

If you cross this obstacle too, then your loved ones come in front of you. Responsibility for family and to accomplish their need also kill your dreams.

Another reason, if a person tried to achieve his dream but got failure, he gave up on his dream. I do not understand one thing why people think failure is the opposite of success. Rather failure is the part of success.

If your dream got blurred or you have not any dream then find out it in form of purpose because *"life without dreaming is a life without meaning."*

How to find your purpose?

I believe that everyone who comes to this planet takes birth for a unique purpose. All their purpose lies within. Those who find out their purpose and dedicate their life becomes extraordinary. The Best way to find out the purpose that lies within you is visualization.

Visualization

If you do not have any dream in your life then do not worry. Just close your eyes, take a deep breath and ask yourself while closing your eyes; what do you like most? What gives you happiness and peace? After few tries you will get your answer. That answer will be the your purpose. But you have to be patient because it can take days, weeks, or months.

You know what, when I don't understand anything in my life or I am not able to find out any answer or solutions to my problems I start visualizing. It might seems boring to you but this is the ultimate and I will say the most powerful secret of all the greats. Whenever I visualize I got my answers every time.

I know many of you will not digest it. But in the beginning, I too could not digest it. When you will see that all the inventions around you are because of visualization or Imagination only, then you will also start believing in the power of visualization.

A famous Scientist Albert Einstein once said "Imagination is more important than the knowledge". knowledge is limited, whereas imagination embraces the entire world.

If you do not know what to visualize just visualize the dream that you want to achieve.

> "*If you can imagine it, you can create it. If you can dream it, you can become it. - William Arthur Ward* "

When you start visualizing your dream, your purpose, or anything else you start connecting to the universe. When you practice it regularly you connect to the direct source of knowledge.

Ask yourself — "Am I ready to die?"

Any day can be the last day of your life. So ask a question to yourself — *"Am I ready to die?"*

I know, answer of the most people will be no. No matter how many policies you take, there is still fear in your mind that what will happen to my family after me? How many days will they survive with the money of that policy and with some savings?

I have seen such a crisis when the only earning member from that family went away. But if someone has made a system, then after his death, his family does not have to face troubles. Understand the sense of urgency because it will give you a purpose that will help in system building.

> "*If you don't find a way to make money while you sleep, you will work until you die. - Warren Buffett*"

Everyone has limited time and we cannot waste time in silly things. We need to understand the sense of urgency. It doesn't matter if you don't have any purpose or dream in your life. But family is your responsibility. You can probably be satisfied with the money earned at this time, but you must ask yourself again and again, "am I ready to die?"

In a job, you are never ready to die? You can ready only you make the system so that it can give money for a lifetime to your family after the death also. Don't depend on life insurance policies. Build your system.

Don't just Be Ambitious

It's good to be ambitious about your future. But think for a moment about what you are ambitious about? Imagine your life by forwarding 10 - 20 years to where you want to reach. Do you find yourself happy? Or take a look at their life whom's like you want to be. Maybe their life looks good from the outside but might be their inside story is something else.

Sometimes we make our purpose of life by looking at other's life or by the influence of society. There is no attachment with that purpose but you are ambitious to get that. Finally, you reach there also but do not find yourself happy. The reason is that was not your purpose it was just a goal that you choose by influence.

Just a few days ago I had a conversation with a friend of mine. After doing his Ph.D., he got a job in a university office. The university gave him the post which a professor gets but he is an associate professor. He was happy that he got a senior post and people older than him also call him Sir.

University kept him super busy and take double work in exchange for peanuts. But he is under the illusion that the university is giving him importance. He has so hectic schedule that even he has no time on weekends for himself and he calls himself ambitious.

Now you tell me whether the university is giving importance to him or is it taking more work for less money. We become so blind in the work that we do not even understand whether what is happening to us is right or not. By the time it will be understood, but it will be too late. That's why after retirement, many people regret that they wasted their life in exchange of some peanuts. As I shared the story of squirrel in the beginning of this book.

"*Don't invest in everyone else's dream and ignore your own.*"

Be ambitious to achieve your purpose, not to achieve others' purpose. In a job, you are ambitious to achieve the company's purpose, not yours.

Beware from Dream Stealer

If you ask a child to write down his dreams, he will write many dreams which he wants to achieve. It was yours as well, but as you grew up, those dreams disappeared somewhere. The society around us stole them.

A person forgets the dream of his life and gets engaged in achieving the goals stated by society. Here, by society I mean your parents, relatives, friends, and teachers.

Society tells us that human beings' only purpose is to find a job after education. Your dreams are just a fantasy, it has nothing to do with reality.

Society's perception of normal is - get up, go to work, come back home, eat, watch TV, then sleep and then repeat for 40 to 50 years.

When time passes, dreams die, and what remains? An old withered body who is sad for what it could do but couldn't.

The world around you is full of very negative people. Whenever you think of doing something and are very excited about it, they will stop you with their doubts and disbeliefs. Like "this won't work", "One of my relatives did it too, but he failed", "Why bother? Do your job and be happy".

They are the dream stealer.

Negative people, friends, family, or coworkers are like a dark cloud. Defend yourself or suffer the consequence of slow assimilation to mediocrity. When you turn your back on these people you stop listening to them.

Positive people nurture your growth, soothe your failures, and invest in your dreams. Associate with such people. Join the community that talks about ideas. Start attending motivational seminars. Ally yourself with like-minded people. Read books and autobiographies of those who have the kind of success you want. Find a mentor who can guide you.

> "*When you stop listening to the world — the world start listening to you.*"

Often people also say that when the pocket is empty, then one should not dream. First, do a job, earn money and save it, then think about the dream after retirement. You need to be beware of these dream stealers. One should dream only when the pocket is empty so that after the pocket is full, they can be fulfilled.

CHAPTER TEN

DECISION AND COMMITMENT

"A dream doesn't become reality through magic. It takes decision and commitment. - Saurabh Goel"

According to research, it is found that the major reason for failure is lack of decision. Most people have dreams, they have ideas, they know what will be right for them but they are unable to make the decisions.

Some reasons I shared in the previous chapter like fear of failure, the responsibility of loved ones, doubt that created by society, self-doubt, and the "How to factor" that means how all things will sort out. But you know, what is the big reason why most people are not able to make a decision? — Because of the Comfort zone!

Comfort Zone

Humans are the creatures of habits. Whatever work he does continuously creates neural pathways in the brain. These neural pathways become patterns of his thoughts and behaviors. These thoughts and behaviors create some boundaries in the mind. Whenever a person tries to cross these boundaries he feels unsafe. These boundaries are nothing just is his Comfort Zone.

The comfort zone is a psychological state in which a person operates in an anxiety-neutral state, using a limited set of behaviors to provide a stable level of performance, usually without a sense of risk. A person feels safe in his Comfort zone and feels like he has some control over the situation. All his immediate needs are met and he feels at peace. That's the reason he is not able to decide because his comfort zone pulls him back.

When a person leaves his comfort zone, he has no longer in a familiar and controllable situation. His brain hasn't built up the pathways necessary to know how to react and he can feel anxiety and fear.

Your parents took all the decisions from childhood, then some decisions of life you took after seeing your friends or by taking the advice of someone else. That's made a habit of not taking decisions on own. A person became so habitual that he even take the opinions of others to buy a car for himself, or which school he should for their children. Now think about how he can make some big decisions of his own. His comfort zone stops him.

A person who is so much habitual of living in a comfort zone analyses things more. I believe, those who analyze more never make decisions.

> "*"You cannot be committed to your dream and comfort zone."*"

You are one decision away from a completely different life. When you decide to do something even after you don't know how it will turn out, but you stay committed to your decision, you start getting the resources too.

I wanted to write a book. But I did not have any Idea about How I will write it? Who will edit it? Who will publish it? And How will it reach the people?

But you know what, the day I decided to write a book and committed myself to launch the book a particular day, I start getting the ideas and resources. I wrote the book, the book got published and the worldwide sale is also happening. And you are reading this book too.

> "*Don't be afraid to start, be afraid to spend 30 to 40 years working for someone else. - Saurabh Goel*"

This is the power of decision. Someone told me one thing that if a person decides that he wants to become a criminal, then he starts getting gun sellers as soon as he goes out of the room. Try to understand the message behind this statement.

When you decide to do something you start meeting with like-minded people, start getting vendors, people related to it.

You can have mediocre comfort now or meteoric comfort later.

Making Excuses on Past References

People make excuses for past references and stop themselves in decision-making. Most of the time their statements are — "You don't know what happened to me in the past."

The universe does not care about your past. Past is blind to the universe. The universe has no memory, only you do. If the universe does not remember, why should you?

If you are defined by your past, it will be impossible for you to become who you need to be in the future.

Just because you failed at anything in past does not mean you will fail again in the future. People often make their perception of the events that happened in the past. If anybody failed at five relationships does not mean your next will fail, especially if you didn't learn from them.

3 Types of People

1. Lovers

The first type of people is lovers. Most motivational speakers say do what you love. People start doing what they love. After some time love fades away. As soon as the love ends, he does not feel like doing the work which he started.

This is because you feel excitement for anything you love when you do it occasionally. But when you start doing that work daily, the excitement ends, and love too.

If you have no excitement, no goal, no reason, no passion mostly probably you will give on the work you love. This is the reason 90% of startups fail in the initial 5 years. Then 90% of the rest of startups fail in the next 5 years. Because the people who started were a lover.

2. Linear

The second type of people is linear. A linear person is dependent on someone else. Always in complaining, crying, and creeping mode. He does not take ownership.

If something is said to them, they will do it, otherwise, they do not take any responsibility on their own. If something goes wrong, they are at the forefront of blaming others.

If they are not able to become anything in life or do not do anything, then they put all their blame on parents or conditions, or society, or on government or system.

Often you will see that people depend on the government after doing their degree. They feel that if we have studied, then the government becomes responsible to give them jobs. A linear person can't start any business because he depends on the system so much than how he can build his system.

These people seek the easy life yet want someone else to pay for it. They believe the government should do more for them. They are victims of the system. They vote for whatever politician promises them the world at no cost. Free health care. Free education. Free gas. Free electricity. Free food.

Taking responsibility is the first step to taking the driver's seat of your life.

3. Leaders

The third type of people is leaders. They are the most impactful people. Leaders always lead by example. They lead from the front. They have commitments for their dream and give consistent efforts until they achieve their goal.

Their purpose creates excitement and passion for the work. That's the reason they refuse to give up. If you want to be an entrepreneur you have to be a leader. You have to come out from the lovers and liners category. Stop complaining and blaming. Take the ownership. Build your system rather dependent on other's systems.

> "*Responsibility is the price of greatness. -Winston Churchill*"

Some people try to motivate you for your dreams but I tell you motivation also does not work to accomplish your dreams. You need some practical theories that work. So I am sharing a practical theory that is the secret of all the legends, Inventors, businessmen.

Commitment - The Ultimate Secret to Success

There is a profound difference between interest and commitment. It is defined by the quality and consistency of your actions. An interested person always says he wants to start a business, on the other hand, a committed person works for it.

Interest is quitting after the first or second failure; commitment is continuing after the hundredth. Thomas Edison never gave up even after the 10000 times failure because of his commitment to making a light bulb.

Wright brothers who invented the plane took multiple attempts and around16 years to make a successful flight.

You pick up the story of any genius and see that no one has succeeded in one go. You think they were geniuses so they have different minds or some extraordinary talent. No, they just know one thing that tries until you get the success.

One more thing, when you want something with a true heart, then the whole universe also tries to get you to meet it. You start finding the ways, people, resources that require for it.

What do you think scientists have all the resources before deciding to go on the moon? The answer is no. They just decide to go to the moon and they start getting the resources and they made it successful.

People interpret the word ‘commitment’ differently. Like people think commitment means sticking yourself with something or making a trap from which it becomes difficult to escape or someone thinks commitment means trying hard.

Commitment means sticking with your decision and being willing to do whatever it takes to accomplish your dream. "Whatever it takes" does not mean unethical or illegal actions. It means never give up. If your dream needs to take 5 steps take 5 steps. If it needs to take 50 steps take those 50 steps. If it needs to take 500 steps take those 500 steps but never give up.

Commitment is the ultimate secret of success because in the story of all the successful people you will find one thing common is commitment.

All the inventions and discoveries are the results of commitment and persistent efforts.

Persistence

Another thing that requires commitment is Persistency. Those, who have cultivated the habit of persistence seem to enjoy insurance against failure. No matter how many times they are defeated, they finally arrive up toward the top of the ladder.

Whatever has been achieved in this world, he has done it because of his stubbornness. Willingness to make your dream come true. Whether it is the stubbornness to go to the moon, or the determination to build a car, or the insistence on connecting the whole world to the Internet. Persistence gives you the mindset of never giving up.

There is an old proverb that "A rolling stone gathers no moss". If you are not persistent and keep changing your focus then you will never get any results. If you want results then be consistent and persistent.

Most people are not able to decide when to start? In this confusion, they keep postponing their decisions on tomorrow.

Do It Now!

Some people do delay in taking the action. When you got an idea you also get motivation with it. You get excited to see the results.

You know what, motivation and excitement are temporary. They don't last forever. Motivation and excitement are like fresh milk: it has an expiration date.

People usually say they will start someday. They always make excuses like I am waiting for the right time. I am waiting for the new year. I am waiting for some money to come. I am waiting to be debt-free. I am waiting for this and I am waiting for that.

My friend that someday is never come. There is no perfect time to start. You have to start now. Stop making excuses do it now.

If you want to do something, you have to do it now. You can't just put it on a shelf and wait two months for it to come around. You can't say that you will do it later. Afterward, you won't be any more excited about it.

If you're motivated and excited about your idea on Friday, take the weekend pledge and dive into the project. When you have high motivation, you can complete two weeks of work in twenty-four hours.

Motivation is a magical thing, a productivity multiplier. But it won't wait for you. If it grabs you, hold it back and put it to work.

Choice

Changing your life starts with changing choices. It isn't one choice but hundreds. And when you line a string of choices together, they create your process, and your process will create your lifestyle. Lifestyle choices will make you a millionaire. People do not choose to be poor. They make poor decisions that slowly assemble into a poorness.

> "*Destiny is not determined by chance but it's determined by the choice you make.*"

You have two choices — one, enjoy today suffer later, and work 40 years to live 10 to 20 years. Second, sacrifice today enjoy later for whole life and work 5 to 10 years to live 40 to 50 years.

If you are not where you want to be, the problem is your choices. *Make a choice — Choice to be an employee or choice to be an entrepreneur.*

If you chose to be an entrepreneur then take action. Because the distance between your dreams and reality is called action.

You know what, even after all these — Idea, purpose, decision, commitment, strategies, and action people still get fail. To know the reason let's proceed to the next chapter.

CHAPTER ELEVEN

MINDSET

"Once your mindset changes, everything on the outside will change along with it. - Steve Maraboli"

After reading all the chapters if you think by just simulating all the things you will become rich, then I will say you are wrong. Most people failed even after implementing all the strategies. Because they Ignore one thing that is the Mindset. Mindset is the key that makes a difference between ordinary and extraordinary.

I remember an anecdote that I heard in a seminar. This is the story of India's very famous and richest businessman Dhirubhai Ambani. I found that story very interesting and inspirational.

Dhirubhai Ambani in his early days in Mumbai use to take evening walks with his friends near the Gateway of India and during the evening walk, he wanted to go to Taj Hotel for a cup of tea.

At that time a cup of tea at the Taj cost around 50 Bucks and only the famous and rich could afford it. When Mr. Ambani starts earning 100 bucks he starts spending his 50 bucks for that cup of tea.

His friends were surprised to see this act of drinking expensive tea in a luxury hotel. Because he can drink tea on the roadside by spending only 5 bucks. Why he is spending the extra 45 bucks?

One day a friend of Dhirubhai asked him the reason for paying so much for a cup of tea.

Dhirubhai replied — "I am paying 5 bucks for tea and another 45 bucks for the mindset. The most influential people in the city come there. It's not about the tea; It's about developing the mindset that these people carry."

This is a crazy and laudable approach towards success. The nature of the thought process sometimes indicates the future of the personality.

It is not necessary to be most skillful or intelligent to become rich, but it is very important to have a mindset. A rich mindset makes you rich and a poor mindset makes you poor. You will see the most common thing in all successful people is the never-give-up mindset. They refuse to give up even in a difficult time.

Read books, read the biography of successful people. Just try to study and observe the mindset of these people.

If you want extraordinary results, you are going to need an extraordinary mindset. Unfortunately, extraordinary is not found in society's mediocracy and the belief that fuels them.

Mindset includes your belief, your attitude, most important change. You should have the mindset of always learning to change. Change is important because a journey from employment to entrepreneurship required different you at different stages.

Change

"*Things do not change; we change. - Henry David Thoreau*"

Most people wait to change the situation or they think when their time will change they will also change.

I always used to think that when I become rich, I will adopt good habits. Like getting up early in the morning, reading books, adopting a rich lifestyle, doing meditation, etc.

Other people like me think that when money will come, they will change. People who think like this never change. It can also be said that those who have such thinking never get any money.

The truth is when you change your mindset and your time also change. Do not wait to change your situation just change your mindset.

Live like you are already an entrepreneur. I am not saying to start spending unnecessarily on things that are not needed at present time. I am saying just to change your mindset. Even if there are no millions of dollars in the pocket, then the walk should be as if there are millions in the pocket.

There is a wonderful saying — *"fake it until you make it."*

You need to change a few things like your mindset, your habits, your behavior, and your lifestyle.

You can't work with an employee mindset. This means if you will have a job mindset you can never come into the 5 % club. You have to change your habits that do not fit. Adopt the habit of learning.

Most importantly change your association. Your association decides your behavior, your mindset. If you live in an association that talks about people more than the ideas then you are in a very wrong association. Those always talk about parties and all then again you are into the wrong association.

It is believed that your annual income will be the average of people you hang out with. Even in childhood, we have been told to be in good company.

As I gave the example of Dhirubhai Ambani. He spent 10 times the price on the cup of tea just for the association.

When you will change your association then you will start changing automatically. You will feel the change in your behavior, your mindset, in your talk, in your walk. You will find different you.

Empty Your Cup

You need to empty your cup every time so that you can fill in new knowledge. Just as by pouring something in a full cup, everything gets scattered outside, in the same way, knowledge in the mind. People think that they already know a lot, because of this, when someone tells a new thing, then it instead of going into the mind, it keeps spreading outside.

What you know today is not enough to get you where you need to be tomorrow. You must constantly reinvent yourself, and reinvention is education. Unfortunately, while infinite knowledge surrounds us, most people ignore it.

People usually say they do have not time to read books. I will say this is an excuse.

Education didn't end with graduation, it started. People think that after reading so many books in college, what to read now. In college, you have not read the book that you need to be. You know what, best leaders are the readers. Many of the top successful entrepreneurs are known to be voracious readers. Microsoft founder, Bill Gates, reads about 50 books a year.

Skills and expertise are waiting just for you. No one drops a book on your lap and gifts knowledge. You have to seek it, process it, and then use it. The acquisition and application of knowledge will make you rich.

Elon musk learned rocket science by reading books. And today he has revolutionized rocket science. I got the confidence of writing a book only by reading many books.

Perception

I have often heard people say whenever they see an expensive car or any expensive item that they will never be able to afford one of these. This is not that they will never able to afford expensive things but their choice of perception is poor. Because of it, they would forever lead him to mediocre results.

Your words make your belief. If you use words like *"I never", "I can't", If only"*. It is true for your mind and it makes your belief you can't and you never will.

Use words *"It's possible", "I will overcome", "I will", "I can".*

Mindset For Adoptability

You need to adopt new things according to time. If you do not change or you do not adopt change your growth will be zero or it will be in minus. There are few examples like Myspace, Yahoo, Orkut, Nokia, blackberry, Kodak, Xerox, and blockbuster these companies failed because they did not adopt the change. Despite being a big brand, their revenue kept falling and today no one even knows them. They become history because they have not changed according to time.

You need to adopt the new things according to the requirement of time and public need. People want an update. That's the reason every electronic, automobile, software company brings new versions and new technology every year. If they will not adopt the change then another company will take over the market.

Attitude

In my journey, I learned one thing is Attitude is Everything. To become successful you required 1 % mechanics and 99 % attitude. When you change your attitude you begin to see new possibilities. You move into action. You achieve extraordinary results. That's why I am saying, it's all about attitude — 99 % attitude and only 1 % mechanics.

It is a little difficult to maintain a positive attitude consistently but if you maintain it no one can stop you to become what you want.

If you are getting confused about what I mean by attitude then I give you an example — If a person says "I can't". His attitude is negative. If a person says "I can". His attitude is positive.

A person with a positive attitude see always positive in everything. If anything bad happens with him he never complains he always feels grateful. He adopts the attitude of gratitude.

By the way, I have used the phrase "this is the secret of success" multiple times in this book. In actual every part of this book is the secret of success. I am using this phrase again for 'Gratitude'.

Gratitude is the secret of success. There are many books on Gratitude that explain its power and no one can deny gratitude is the ultimate secret of success.

Stop blaming and stop complaining just start seeing positive in everything. Learn from the child who is learning to walk. When a child walks he stumbles and falls. But you will never see him blaming his parents or the floor. He does not quit. He gets up again and makes another attempt. He keeps going with a positive attitude until he learns to walk.

If you have never been able to do anything in life, do not blame it on someone else. Take responsibility and see what's wrong you did. Correct that mistake and move forward. Anytime you fall get up again.

Once upon a time, a man would always say 'the world is dirty' while looking through his glass window. One day his friend came and saw that the mirror was covered with dust. He cleaned it up and then everything looked good to the man.

Got my point? if you are seeing anything bad in anyone then clean your window. You need to change your perception and your attitude then you start seeing good in everything.

"When you combine a positive attitude with the other success principles, you become unstoppable." - Jeff Keller

Mindset of Belief

You know what, this is the most important topic of this book. I am talking about this in the last because you may forget the initial content but I want you must remember this. It often happens that we forget the initial things, but we mostly remember what was read in the last.

I am talking about belief. If you have not believed in your dream, in your idea and have some doubts then it is a little difficult for you to accomplish it. You can't say I have 99 percent belief and only 1 percent doubt. Belief should be 100 percent.

A single drop of black into a bucket of white can change the colour of white. The same 1 percent of doubt can change your belief system.

If you applied all the principles of success but without believing in these then all vanish. Even if you take the medicine of the doctor without belief, then it also does not work. Your subconscious mind works on one principle that is belief.

Whatever your subconscious mind accepts it is true for him. If a person repeats a lie over and over, his subconscious mind eventually accepts the lie as truth. Moreover, he will believe it to be the truth.

If you convince your subconscious mind of anything it will start attracting possibilities for it. Thomas Edison did not give up even after 10000 failures because he convinced his subconscious mind for success and he had believed that he will get success. Finally, he got success.

Scientists had believed that they will go to the moon one day. The result is in front of us.

20 or 30 years ago, things were impossible for people, but some people had believed in themselves, today they have made those things possible. Whether to connect the whole world to the Internet, to go to space and other discoveries in science.

All are the results of someone's belief. Think if anyone because of whom we can take advantage of any facility, if he does not believe in his idea, then we may not be able to take advantage of that facility.

> “*"Don't be afraid to step out of the crowd and chase your dreams. Believe in yourself."*”

When the Wright brothers started working for the airplane, people spoke to them a lot. Like you guys are foolish. You are wasting your time because flying a machine is impossible. How could something so heavy float in the air? Law of physics — Gravity will not allow anything to fly in the sky.

After listening to all this, a normal person might give up. Because his belief system will be shaken. But wright brothers were not the ordinary they were extraordinary. Their beliefs were also extraordinary that didn't shake.

In the same way, *"extraordinary wealth will require you to have extraordinary beliefs."*

Mindset of Never Give Up

There are very few people who dare to face their fears, who believe in their dreams and their ideas. There are few people who make decisions, who are committed, and have the determination to get things done. There are very few people who maintain a positive attitude. There are few people who go through the journey towards entrepreneurship and refuse to give up.

You can also be one of those few people. You have the potential to become more than you ever dreamed of. You have greatness within you. You just need one click to start up.

I have seen people usually give up when they do not see early results. Sometimes it takes time to show you results. For that, you need to be consistent.

I have a lot of examples that I experienced in my life to explain it. But I am sharing one example that you can also try by yourself.

One day I was trying to make a whipped coffee. For that, you need to beat coffee with sugar by adding little water. When you beat you do not get early results. For a moment it comes to mind to give up and make simple coffee. But when you beat it consistently then it starts showing the results.

Those already tried can understand it or those who do not try, try it. All the motivation and learnings are around you. You just need to be an observer.

Starting your own business is like riding a roller coaster. There are highs and lows and every turn you take is another twist. The lows are low, but the highs can be high. You have to be strong, keep your stomach tight, and ride along with the roller coaster that you started. - Lindsay Manseau, photographer, and entrepreneur

What if Someone fail?

There may be a question in your mind — "Saurabh, What if someone gets the failure even after trying so much consistently?"

As I said become an observer your surroundings will give you an answer automatically. When you spend time with nature it helps you in learning a lot of things.

Nature taught me the most important lessons of my life. That is "*Slow is Fast, Fast is Slow. Slow success builds character. Fast success builds ego.*"

A plant that grows fast initially there is a chance will fall quickly. The reason for this is its roots and its stem. When the tree grows fast in the beginning, its root will not be so strong and its stem will also be weak and thin. Because of this, it will fall into a storm.

But when a tree grows slowly its root becomes strong and its stem also becomes strong. There are very less chances it will fall easily in a storm. When it established its roots then it starts growing fast.

> "*Early success is a scam.*"

Whoever has said this, he is somewhere said in this context that early success teaches you nothing. It builds ego in you. But failures teach you real lessons. This makes your root stronger. When you get success after some failures it makes you humble and you have a lot of learning about how to behave in challenging situations.

There is a tree in my garden. When it was growing, monkeys came and climbed on its twig and broke it. It grew again and the monkeys broke it again. Don't know how many times it was broken but that tree didn't give up.

In the meantime, its main stem became thick and strong. Now it is growing strongly and beautifully. Now there is no effect of playing monkeys climbing on it.

Do not be afraid of failure. Failures are not the opposite of success. These are the part of success. Failures make you stronger. Whenever you get any failure take it as a blessing and come back strongly more than before.

There may be a delay in your success but what's you do, what's you speak and what is your mindset during the delay will decide how long this delay will last.

I hope this book inspired you and you will share this book with others also. Now is the time to start your journey towards entrepreneurship that can create miracles in your life and others' lives too.

Make your mindset, believe in yourself, and follow your dreams. If you have made any system as I shared in this book, then teach it to other people.

Teach...not just Give

Not just give money to the next generation teach them how to make money. If you give a fish to a person he will eat it in one day. If you teach him how to do fishing he will eat his whole life.

Thanks for reading and may God bless you on your journey.

Teach...not just

About The Author

Saurabh Goel is the founder and CEO of Training and Counselling Company 'Brain Soul & You'. For more than 5 years, he delivered presentations on entrepreneurship, mind programming, and motivation.

He did his B.tech in IT and later choose to be a successful psychologist. He is helping people in various ways by his counselling and training sessions. To contact him, send a email to saurabhgoel@brainsoulnyou.com

Learn more at brainsoulnyou.com

Printed by Libri Plureos GmbH in Hamburg,
Germany